Sydney Travels to Venice

A Guide for Kids

Let's Go to Italy Series!

First Edition

ISBN: 978-1-60145-983-1

Printed in the United States of America.

Sydney's Travel Guides for Kids
2009

All photographs by Cheri Svagerko and Keith Svagerko

Sydney's Travel Guides for Kids
www.SydneysTravelGuidesforKids.com

Email: travel@sydneystravelguidesforkids.com

Dedicated to Kids around the World

A Note from Sydney

Hi, my name is Sydney. I love to travel to new places with my mom and dad. Italy is great, and Venice is one of my favorite places in Italy. Before we went to Venice my dad read lots of travel guides, but we could not find one just right for me. My dad and I decided to write this travel guide for kids so that you will know what to expect in Venice and hopefully have as much fun as I did. Since my dad is a grown-up, he did most of the writing, but he could not have done it without me since I am a kid—and this is a kid's guide! I hope you have fun. Please send me an email at travel@sydneystravelguidesforkids.com and let me know what you liked best about Venice.

Ciao, Sydney

A Note from Keith

Yes, Sydney and I agree that kids deserve travel guides too. We hope this guide prepares you for a super trip to Venice. We don't share everything about Venice in this guide. Your grown-ups will probably have plenty of their own travel guides and maps and they can fill you in where we leave off. We do share with you many of the sights we think are great and that we enjoyed. We hope that we prepare you just a little for the amazing things you will see and for the fun you will have. Congratulations, you are one of few lucky kids that actually get to go to Venice and know something about it before you arrive! You might want to thank your grown-ups for the trip to Venice as well as for this guide made just for you, and be sure to have lots of fun!

Arrivederchi, Keith

Table of Contents

Arriving: This is Venice for Kids

No streets, no cars, lots of water and boats *everywhere*. Speed boats, slow boats, bus boats, fire boats, mail boats, police boats, trash boats, ferry boats, tow boats, and long black beautiful sleek boats called **Gondolas**. Venice is known for its Gondolas and the men who make them go—they are called **Gondoliers**. There are boats just about everywhere you look. In fact, we think there is no better way to enter Venice than by water as people have done for centuries. The Water Taxi is a great, but expensive, way to get to Venice from the airport. Once in Venice, have your grown-ups buy a pass and be prepared to hop on and off a motorized boat called a **Vaporetto**. Vaporetti are like city busses with convenient stops all over the city and the nearby islands of **Murano**, **Burano, Torcello** and the **Lido**, but if you get off between stops you *will* get very wet!

Once thought of as the richest place in the world, Venice is a city of grand and famous **palaces and churches**. Many of the city's amazing palaces are found along the **Grand Canal** that winds its way through the city. You can visit several of these palaces as well as the palace where the ruler of Venice lived called the **Doge's Palace.** Other neat palaces include the more modern **Ca' Rezzonico**, now a museum displaying life from Venice in the 1700's. No trip to Venice would be complete without seeing some of the most beautiful churches in the whole world. **St. Mark's Church**, located in **St. Mark's Square**, is one of the most spectacular of all!

In addition to all of its boats, palaces and churches, Venice is known for its celebrations. One of the largest celebrations is called the **Carnival**. Now, this is not like the carnival back home, this is a huge masked party! Since Venice is known for this large masked party, you are going to see lots of really neat handmade Carnival **masks**. If you want, you can visit a mask making factory and watch them being made. Surely one of these masks will be just the right size for you!

You will also see a variety of pretty **colored glass** made on the nearby world famous island of **Murano**. Murano glass was known for hundreds of years as the best glass in the world and many glass making secrets have been handed down from generation to generation. Many of the glass factories give tours and demonstrations that you can watch. You are going to *love* Venice! It is an exciting water adventure with so much water and really neat bridges, so wear comfortable shoes and get ready to explore an enchanting city in a big lagoon.

A City in a Big Lagoon

Venice sits right in the middle of an enormous lagoon and has a famous history. Have you ever heard of Marco Polo? Marco Polo was from the big lagoon! When he was just a teenager, he set out with his father to the East and visited far away lands. When he returned more than 20 years later he wrote all about his journey. This was the first time most people had ever heard about these far away lands of the East and his adventure eventually opened new trading routes between the West and the East. He would probably be proud to know that many kids around the world remember his name when playing in the swimming pool.

This collection of islands in a big lagoon that we call Venice is a water wonderland really made up of more than 100 islands and more than 200 canals. It is just about 3 feet above sea level and sometimes you may get your feet wet. In fact, the city often places benches in St. Mark's Square for people to walk on when the water is high, especially in the fall and winter.

Winding right down the center of Venice is the Grand Canal. Here, amazing palaces and churches have been built in the mud! That's right; all of these building are built on trees driven into the mud! Over time, the trees petrified and became solid rock to provide a good foundation. The trees that were driven into the mud actually turned into rock! The early Venetians cleared many forests to create their foundations in the lagoon. Still, some of the buildings are slowly leaning and sinking! Don't worry though; they should still be standing by the time you arrive.

When visiting the beautiful city of Venice we highly recommend that you visit lots of neat places like palaces, churches, museums, and other islands in the lagoon. Take time to walk along the canals and see the people who live in Venice. Tourists love Venice and they always have. Get ready for lots of fun as you really enter another world, one that long ago was a super power in the Adriatic Sea and today is a tourist magnet.

Boat Tour of the Grand Canal

Sydney Says...

"Sit outside in the back of the vaporetto, the seats are better and the breeze and views are great!"

There is no better way to see the city than by taking a slow boat ride down the Grand Canal. Usually people start the tour from the Piazzale Roma, or train station, and end at San Marco, or St. Mark's Square. You can also go the other direction. We think the slower # 1 vaporetto boat is the best way to go as you make your way along the lovely 2 ½ mile canal that divides the city in half. But if you are in a hurry you can still travel the Grand Canal on the faster # 82 Vaporetto.

Along the way to St. Mark's Square you will see old interesting palaces like **Ca' Rezzonico, Ca' Pesaro and Ca' d'Oro** that line the canal. You will also see famous bridges that cross the canal including the famous **Rialto Bridge**. A lot of people try to sit near the front or near the entrances of the vaporetto to get a good view of these palaces and bridges, but Sydney says "sit outside in the very back, the seats are better and the breeze and views are great!" Strike up a conversation with a local.

The Gondola Ride

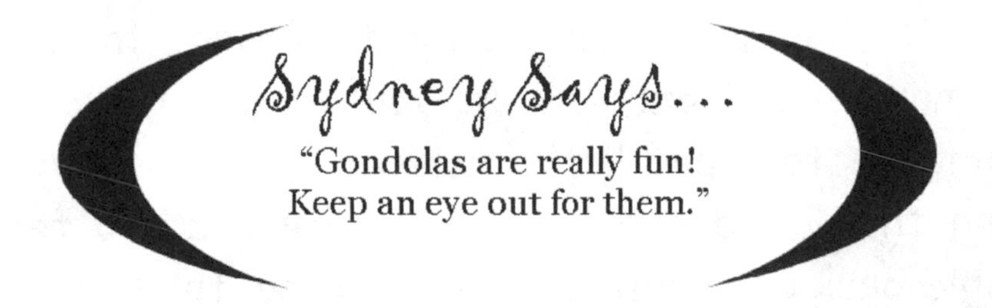

Sydney says "I recommend a gondola." Encourage your grown-ups to save some money now for a gondola ride. Like the **Water Taxi**, it is a kind of expensive way to see parts of Venice, but Sydney says "I love the gondola and it is worth it." We think the best place for a gondola ride is along the smaller more narrow canal routes, away from the busy larger water ways.

While the small canals are wonderful, have your grown-ups ask your gondolier to include the Rialto Bridge area in your ride, preferably in the early evening. The night time gondola ride can be one of the most memorable experiences of your visit. Along the way, look for cats sitting along the sides of the canal watching the evening activities. All in all, the grace of the gondola sliding quietly across the still evening water is magical.

Now, if your grown-ups really don't want to spend the money on a gondola ride, you can still get a nice short one for very little money. At certain spots along the Grand Canal, gondolas are used to ferry people back and forth across the canal for less than the price of an ice cream (gelato) cone. These crossings are referred to as traghetti crossings. You have to stand up for these short rides, but they can be fun too and give you a chance to be in a real gondola. Since you have to stand up, you might want to hold your grown-up's hand so that you will not lose your balance. Look for small yellow signs, or find a local map for the locations, and enjoy your gondola ride!

Gondolas used to be the only way people traveled around Venice. They also used to be decorated and painted in wild colors, but it became so competitive between gondoliers that they were ordered to paint them all black, and they have remained that way for hundreds of years.

Neat Places to Visit

St. Mark's Square

St. Mark's Square is also called the Piazza of San Marcos, and it is really quite amazing. It is truly the heart of Venice and the must see location on your visit. This is the place where you will find lots of pigeons, and often some dogs to pet! If you can only go to one place in Venice, go to St. Mark's Square. Here you will find **St. Mark's Church**, th

Doge's Palace, the **Campanile (Bell Tower)** of St. Mark, the **Clock Tower** and the Moors and the **Correr Museum**.

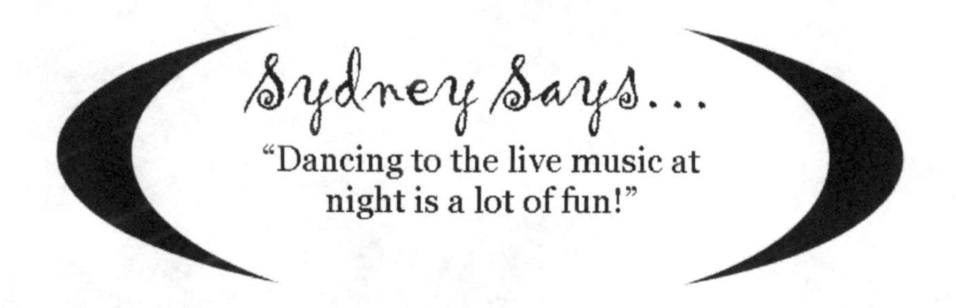

St. Mark's Church

St. Mark's Church, also called San Marcos Basilica, is the oldest church you may ever visit. It was built over a thousand years ago in the 11th century and is the resting place for the bones of St. Mark from the Bible—the city's patron Saint!

How did St. Mark get to Venice? The legend is that two sailors stole the body of St. Mark from the city of Alexandria and brought it to Venice. Notice the lions with wings all over the place? The winged lion is a symbol of St. Mark the evangelist, as well as for the city, and it has been for hundreds of years. St. Mark traveled far to spread the Good News, or the Gospel. You will notice the winged lion has his big paw on an open book representing the Gospels. You will find these magical lions all across Venice and even in countries that were once under the contro of Venice. **How many winged lions can you find?** Send an email to Sydney and let her know the number you found! Afterwards, check our website to see what other kids reported.

St. Mark's Church has five large beautiful domes and is arranged in the shape of a Greek cross. You can see these domes rise above the Doge's Palace. Once inside St. Mark's Church, look up in the domes to see golden mosaics depicting stories from the Bible, such as the story of Adam and Eve and Noah and the Ark. On the walls and floor, you will find rich gold mosaics, colorful tiles and interesting marble patterns everywhere. **Can you find the peacocks?** Early Christian mosaics included peacocks as a symbol of renewal and the resurrection.

As you will see, St. Mark's Church is the home of some ancient treasures. One such treasure is an altar screen of gold covered in beautiful jewels. Another treasure to be on the lookout for is four ancient bronze horses called the *Horses of San Marcos*. These are located upstairs in the San

Marcos Museum. These horses are very, very old and have traveled to very interesting places. These horses were made during the time of Alexander the Great way back in the 4th century B.C., if not earlier. Like the gold altar screen, these horses are believed to have been brought to Venice from the spectacular ancient city of Constantinople. Constantinople was the home of the Emperor Constantine and the capital of the Eastern Roman Empire!

You may notice that St. Mark's Church looks kind of different than many of the other buildings in Venice. The main style of St. Mark's Church is called "byzantine" and it represents a beautiful combination of western and eastern architecture. In fact, there is much about Venice that tells its history as the crossroads of the West and East. You will see this style in other Venetian buildings inspired by artists from the East.

Doge's Palace

Sydney Says...

"Have fun at the Doge's Palace but don't get in trouble...the prison cells are spooky!"

Venice was not a part of Italy until 1866. For much of its long history, it was a very powerful Republic.

This Republic was ruled from the **Doge's Palace**, also called the Ducal Palace, for almost 900 years. The Doge (the ruler of Venice) lived in this huge palace and ruled the country for his whole life. The Doge's Palace was the main location for the government of the Republic. For your tour you will enter the Doge's Palace from the water side, but the main entrance is next to St. Mark's Church and is called the **Porta della Carta**. The Porta della Carta connects St. Mark's Church with the Doge's Palace. Above the Porta della Carta entrance you will see a Doge kneeling before a Winged Lion. This was created to show that the Doge was humble before the patron saint of Venice. Before you get to the entrance, closer to your own eye level, you will see a corner of the building holding an ancient statue of four men called the **Tetrarchs.**

This old statue probably came to Venice from Constantinople during the Crusades and is believed by some to represent four emperors of the Roman Empire.

Once you enter the Porta della Carta you will see a large courtyard with fountains. Directly in front of you will be the **Staircase of the Giant**, or sometimes just called the **Giant Steps**.

The Giant Steps are where each new Doge was crowned the ruler of Venice. You can't walk up and down them now, but you can get your picture in front of them! Notice the really large statues at the top? These represent the Roman gods of Mars and

Neptune; the god of war and the god of the sea. These steps were designed to really intimidate foreign visitors to Venice. Imagine these steps leading up to your front door! Surely your neighbors would be impressed, or frightened.

Now climb the stairs for tourists, and as you enter the big hallway, or **loggia**, you will work your way to the grand **Gold Staircase.** It is not as gold as it used to be, but like the Giant Steps, the Gold Staircase was meant to really impress visitors and show the wealth of Venice. Other really cool things to see at the Doge's Palace are the **Armory** and the **Prison**. The armory has really old weapons that were used by the guards of the Republic. You will also see paintings of the grand Venetian fighting forces of the Sea.

The prison of course is where they sent trouble makers sometimes never to be seen again! One really interesting fact is that Venetians could drop off little notes at the Doge's Palace accusing neighbors of breaking the law. These little pieces of paper were placed in a statue of a **Lion's Mouth** on the wall that is still visible today. Everyone knew to be careful about making accusations because the punishment for wrongly accusing people could be greater than the punishment for the reported misdeed! Go down deep in the dungeon and see how thick the doors are—no getting out of there! Sydney says: "Be sure to visit the Doge's Palace, but don't get in trouble, the prison cells are spooky."

As you wind your way through, you will find many, many rooms in the Doge's Palace. Some of the neatest rooms are the **Senate Hall** where laws were made, and the **Hall of the Great Council**, where the Doge was elected. These rooms have oil paintings everywhere, including the world's largest, from very famous Venetian artists such as **Tintoretto**. Look up!

Before you leave the Doge's Palace, be sure to visit the very popular bridge that attaches the Doge's Palace to the new prisons; it is called the **Bridge of Sighs**. From the outside you will probably see lots of people taking pictures of it! It is a part of the eerie dungeons. Supposedly when prisoners were sent to the prison, they took one last look out of the bridge's port holes and sighed as they pondered their last view of the city. Goodbye beautiful Venice!

<u>Tip for Grown-ups</u>: For a behind the scenes story, book a "secret itineraries" tour well before you arrive.

There are two large columns near the front of the Doge's Palace near St. Mark's Basin (the water in front of the Doge's Palace where the gondolas are waiting for passengers). One of the columns has a winged lion representing St. Mark and the other has a statue of St. Theodore with his crocodile or dragon. Before St. Mark's bones were brought to Venice and he was named the city's **patron saint**, St. Theodore had been the city's patron saint. By the way, Sydney thought you would want to know that a patron saint is a special protector, or guardian of the city. Long ago, patron saints brought more fame, and people, to places.

Campanile of St. Mark

Impossible to miss, the large bell tower outside of St. Mark's Church provides a great view of St.

Mark's Square. After several hundred years, the original bell tower collapsed about a hundred years ago. A new one just like it was built in the same spot. It looks just like the old one but this one has an elevator. On a clear day, you can see all the way to the Alps! Look at St. Mark's Church from here to see the Greek cross pattern.

Clock Tower and the Moors

The Clock Tower was built during the Renaissance and has been keeping time for more than five hundred years. At the very top of the tower are two bronze statues of men called Moors. The Moors strike the gong to mark time throughout the day. In addition to telling the time, the Clock Tower provides a zodiac calendar, the seasons and the phases of the moon. You can get a really good, and sometimes long, view of the Clock Tower as you wait in line to enter St. Mark's Church. See the Winged Lion?

Correr Museum

One of our favorite museums in Venice is the Correr Museum. Inside you will find a big gold and silver coin collection spanning the history of Venice. Imagine having all those gold and silver coins!

The Correr has three floors with lots of different kinds of things to see. We like it because of the great variety of items. The armory collection has lots of different weapons like swords, shields, bows and arrows, guns and knives such as those used by the guards of the Doge's Palace. There is a really neat collection of old books, maps and globes that fill many of the rooms. You will surely find something interesting in the Correr Museum! Best of all, it will probably not be very crowded and you will learn much about the history of Venice.

The museum is located on St. Mark's Square on the opposite end from St. Mark's Church. The grown-ups will be happy that the ticket is included in the price to enter the Doge's Palace. When you leave the Correr, you can get a great photo near the entrance with St. Mark's Church in the background.

Tip for Grown-ups: We recommend that you start at the Correr Museum first because it is not very crowded. You can buy your combo ticket to include the Doge's Palace, and you don't have to wait in a long line. The Correr has lots of neat things for adults and kids including a huge coin collection, swords, armour, shields, globes, costumes, shoes, old maps and books. Plus, there are lots of sculptures and paintings. The top floor has an outstanding art gallery that even the grown-ups will love!

Famous Palaces

The Grand Canal is lined with beautiful palaces that were once the homes of wealthy families. Long ago, only the Doge's home was called a palace and many of these palaces were simply referred to as Casa, or Ca' which means "home." These palaces have not changed much over time due to strict requirements by the city to preserve their historical value. Many are now vacant, or are art galleries and museums. While you will find many palaces along the Grand Canal, we will mention just three.

Ca' Rezzonico

This beautiful palace along the Grand Canal is now the site of the Museum of 18th Century Venice. Among a variety of interesting items that show some aspects of the Venetian's grand style of living, you can see paintings from artists such as Canaletto, Guardi, Longhi and Tiepolo. The palace has many beautiful ceiling frescoes (paintings) painted by Tiepolo. Ornate wooden furniture and glass chandeliers from Murano give some idea about the splendid high living that existed here in the 1700's. Famous people have lived and died here. Look for some interesting bed rooms and unfinished art as you visit each floor of this great old mysterious building. Be sure to see the great views outside.

Ca' Pesaro

The *Ca'* Pesaro is one of the distinctive buildings along the Grand Canal representing the Venetian "Baroque" style architecture. Remember the "Byzantine" style of St. Mark's Church? Can you see the differences? It has beautiful decorations and columns and is the home of the Gallery of Modern Art and the Oriental Museum. The Oriental Museum features a collection of Far Eastern art and other cultural items. Some people really like it, others not so much.

Ca' d'Oro

This beautiful golden palace on the Grand Canal is an example of Venetian architecture called a "Gothic" palace. The Gothic style is different than the Byzantine and Baroque. It shares many of the same designs as the Doge's Palace and was built in the early 1400's. The name means "golden house" and it was once covered in gold leaf and brilliant expensive colors. Inside the Ca' d'Oro is a gallery of art and sculpture with paintings from artists including Titian and Tintoretto.

The Rialto Bridge

There are more than 400 bridges in Venice and some are quite famous. Only four cross the Grand Canal and one of them is called the Ponte di Rialto, or the

Rialto Bridge, and it is old and quite popular. It was built more than 500 years ago. It was the only bridge across the grand canal until about 150 years ago! The Rialto Bridge is located at the most narrow place along the Grand Canal and got its name from the words "rivo alto" or "high bank."
The Rialto Bridge area has historically been the commercial center of Venice where fisherman and locals gather for the freshest food on the island. You can still find fresh vegetables, fruits and seafood at the nearby Rialto market.

If you decide to mail a postcard while in Venice, you can easily drop in to the Post Office located next to the Rialto Bridge. While the locals don't want you to sit around on the Rialto Bridge, feel free to visit the shops and take some pictures as you walk across it. You may notice a very nice cool breeze in the evening. The Rialto is a super place to see the Grand Canal.

Churches

Italy has always been home to large beautiful churches and Venice has many of them. We know that spending your time in old churches is probably not all you want to do in Venice, but in addition to St. Mark's Church, we do want to tell you about a couple more. Scattered throughout Venice you will find quite remarkable churches. Many of these are filled with interesting art and the tombs of famous people. Some, such as the San Giorgio Maggiore, provide an opportunity to travel up the bell tower to view the city. Others, such as the Frari church, provide an opportunity to see amazing art and sculptures in the place they were created for viewing. While we will only mention these, feel free to drop in to one of the many churches along your walks to see what each has to offer. Remember as you visit that most of these churches are still used for religious services and ask that you wear appropriate clothing and not use flash photography.

San Giorgio Maggiore

Since it sits across the water from St. Mark's Square, the bell tower at San Giorgio Marjorie provides the very best view of the city. This is an ideal place for pictures and for watching ships come into and out of Venice. The bells still ring, so you might get a big surprise. As you are leaving, see the metal statue that once sat on the top of the bell tower. Take a walk through the church and see where the choir sits.

The Frari Church

Sydney Says...

"Get the audio tour and map to learn all about the sights in the Frari."

The Basilica di Santa Maria Gloriosa dei Frari, or simply the Frari, is a magnificent example of a Gothic style Venetian church. If you can only see one other church besides St. Mark's, we recommend this one. The Frari is undergoing extensive restorations (making it nice again) as well as repairs to the bell tower, which has a large visible crack. The Frari bell tower is the second largest one in Venice. The work they are doing is explained in English on signs in the church providing a very interesting explanation of the scientific approach to repairs and restoration to the tower. The Frari has many interesting sights to see, including art works and tombs. Sydney says "get the audio tour and map to learn all about the sights in the Frari." Highlights include a masterpiece painting on the high altar by the artist, Titian, called *The Assumption.* You will also find that Titian is buried in the Frari. Be sure to look at the neat wooden hand carved choir stalls. **Can you find a wooden statue of John the Baptist created by Donatello, the famous artist from Florence?** If you can, you will have found his only work in Venice.

<u>Tip for Grown-ups</u>: The Frari is very large and there are many highlights. We recommend an audio tour for kids. This is a church that you can easily spend a lot of time in looking around and the audio guide helps keep it interesting for kids.

Museums

Venice has so many museums that it can be hard to decide which ones to visit. While the Correr Museum was our choice, there are several others that you might want to consider visiting. We will tell you about three others that lots of people really enjoy seeing.

Accademia Museum

The Accademia Museum is home to the greatest Venetian art in the world. Here you will find the greatest collection of works from the old Venetian masters. There is a very nice old wooden bridge across the Grand Canal located just outside the Accademia.

Peggy Guggenheim Museum

The Peggy Guggenheim Museum is home to a collection of modern art along with a sculpture garden. Peggy Guggenheim was from America but lived in Venice with her dogs. She had her very own gondola! She died in 1979 and her home and art were donated to Venice to create the museum. The museum provides an area just for children to explore their creative talents.

Naval History Museum

Long before Venice was a part of Italy, it was a powerful Republic. Given its location in the lagoon, Venice was a significant naval power and feared by many. The Naval History Museum provides an excellent display of this naval military history. This museum is all about water craft and has a great replica of the Doge's ride. In addition, it has a very large and interesting seashell collection.

A Visit to Murano Island

Murano is the historical glass capital of the world and is home to Venice's only glass museum. Glass has a long history in Venice. The nearby island of Murano has glass factories and showrooms for viewing really neat art glass as well as trinkets. Just a 10 minute boat ride away, you can reach this lovely island on a vaporetto, but we recommend the water taxi! Some of the glass factories provide a complimentary water taxi ride to their factory. After a short demonstration, you are free to explore the island and make your own way back to Venice on a vaporetto. No matter how you get there, be sure to visit a glass factory to see the skilled artisans making and blowing glass from glowing molten blobs. If you want to find neat small gifts for your friends and family, you will find a treasure trove of glass products to choose from here—including glass paper weights, writing pens, necklaces, bracelets and animals. You can find many neat glass souvenirs at the shops and stands along the main canal in Murano. Before you leave, walk along Murano's grand canal and find the large, really great glass art displays for a memorable photo.

Amazing Art

Venice is home to some of the greatest artwork in the world. Our favorite artwork is the mosaics in St. Mark's Church. These small brilliant tiles were carefully placed by skilled artists to create picture stories. Each dome features different stories from the Bible and were created over several hundred years. You will find great works of art in Venice. Try to find the following three artists whose name begins with the letter "T" when visiting some of the places we have mentioned in this guide. The works of **Tintoretto,** one of the great Venetian masters, can be viewed in the Accademia Museum, the Doge's Palace, San Giorgio Maggiore and Ca' d'Oro. One of several masterpieces by **Titian** is found in the sanctuary of the Frari Church and other works may be viewed in the Ca' d'Oro. Paintings by **Tiepolo** can be seen in the ceiling frescoes of Ca' Rezzonico.

Beaches, Parks & Fountains

Public Beaches

If you have time and want to enjoy some sandy beaches, travel out to the **Lido**. The Lido is an almost 10 mile stretch of beach that forms a barrier between the lagoon and the Adriatic sea. This is a popular beach destination and can be reached by the vaporetto. While much of the beach is private and sometimes crowded, there is a public area called the **Spiaggia Comunale**. This public area is about a 15 minute walk from where the vaporetto drops you off. Rather than the public area, your grown-up may want to rent a cabana at a private section of the beach. The Lido also has bike rentals, so if you and your grown-ups want to go for an enjoyable bicycle ride, plan on taking a boat ride to the Lido.

Public Parks

If you get a little tired of being indoors, there are several parks in Venice. Many of the public parks are rather small and simply offer benches for rest. But you definitely can find some playground equipment at a few! If you want to swing and slide, we recommend the **Giardina Publica,** or **The Public Gardens,** located not too far from the Naval Museum. You can walk or catch the water bus. We recommend visiting after a nice stroll along the water. Just think as you play here that Napoleon created this park so that kids like you would get a break from all the other great stuff in Venice! If you just want to sit down in a park and draw a picture or read, there is one near St. Mark's Square. The **Giardinetti Reali**, or **The Royal Gardens**, provides benches with nice views and is located between St. Mark's Square and St. Mark's basin (the water). This park is close to several stands that offer a variety of souvenirs.

Public Fountains

You will see several drinking fountains throughout Venice. These fountains have small spigots constantly streaming. The fountain water is the same water used inside, is one of the few free things in Venice and is delicious. Fill your bottle!

Awesome Souvenirs & Gifts

Sydney Says...

"A fan is great to cool you down, and there are even pink ones."

The 10 day celebration called the Carnival lead to the creation of interesting **masks**. The masks let some people go out in public and celebrate Carnival without other people knowing who they were. You are going to see lots of really neat handmade Carnival masks. There are even mask making factories that you can visit. Paper Mache, ceramic, plaster and even leather masks are found in the shops throughout the city. These are fun souvenirs and make great gifts.

You will see many places selling a variety of hand held **fans** for cooling you down on a hot summer day. Some of these fans have pictures and writing on them, others have painting. Some are plastic and some are bamboo. Sydney says "a fan is great to cool you down, and there are even pink ones."

Neat Foods

If you like ice cream, **gelato** is one of the most delightful treats to eat in Venice. There are many locations offering this delicious treat and our advice is to try as many as your grown-ups will allow! You will find some most unusual flavors—be brave and try new ones! You can sample flavors before making your choice and deciding, one scoop or two?

You should probably not fill up only on gelato since Venice has some of the best pizza in Italy. Delicious large cheese pizzas are offered in just about every place you might find food and the **margherita pizza** is quite popular with kids. In fact, Sydney says "the margherita pizza is the best!" The pizza is so good that you might be tempted to have it at every meal, but you would miss out on outstanding **pasta**. Spaghetti is just one of the many types of pasta you can enjoy at every meal. Remember that Venice is in a big lagoon, so there are many types of **seafood** for you to try. Since we encourage you to try new foods, we will not tell you what Sydney say's about seafood—try it and let *her know what you say!*

Italian Words to Know

We encourage you to try to learn a few Italian words before you travel to Venice. It makes the visit extra fun because you can speak to some of the locals and maybe even help your grown-ups if they get lost! At least learn some of the basic words below. You will certainly impress the locals and they will definitely appreciate your effort to communicate in their language.

Tip for Grown-ups: We suggest practicing these words together at breakfast or dinner several weeks before the trip to Venice. Not only does it teach kids to value the Italian language, it is a great way to build anticipation and excitement for the trip. We believe that kids love new language experiences.

Yes = Si (see)
No = No (noh)
Thank you = Grazie (grah-tsee-eh)

More Italian Words to Know

You are welcome = Prego (preh-go)
Please = Per favore (pair-fa-vor-eh)
Excuse me = Mi scusi (mee skoo-zee)
I'm sorry = Mi dispiace (mee dee-spee-ah-cheh)
Ice cream = Gelato (jel-lah-toh)
Hello = Ciao (chow)
Good Morning = buon giorno (bwon jor-noh)
Good Evening = buono serra (bwon ah sair-ah)
Good Night = buono notte (bwon ah nout eh)
Where is? = Dove? (doh-veh?)
Do you speak English = Parla inglese (par-lah een-gleh-zeh?)
I don't understand = Non capisco (non ka-pee-skoh)
Okay = Va bene (va beh-neh)
Goodbye = ciao (chow) or arrivederchi (ah-ree-veh-dair-chee)

Tip for Grown-ups: These words may help out if you happen to get lost in Venice. The street signs and numbers can be confusing. If you happen to get lost, simply ask a local "dove San Marcos?" and they will probably point you in the right direction. By the way, Venice is a great city to get lost in. Remember, you are on an island! No matter where your adventures take you in Venice, we hope you have a great time!

Extras: Maps, Puzzles and Word Games

Map: Venice Sites

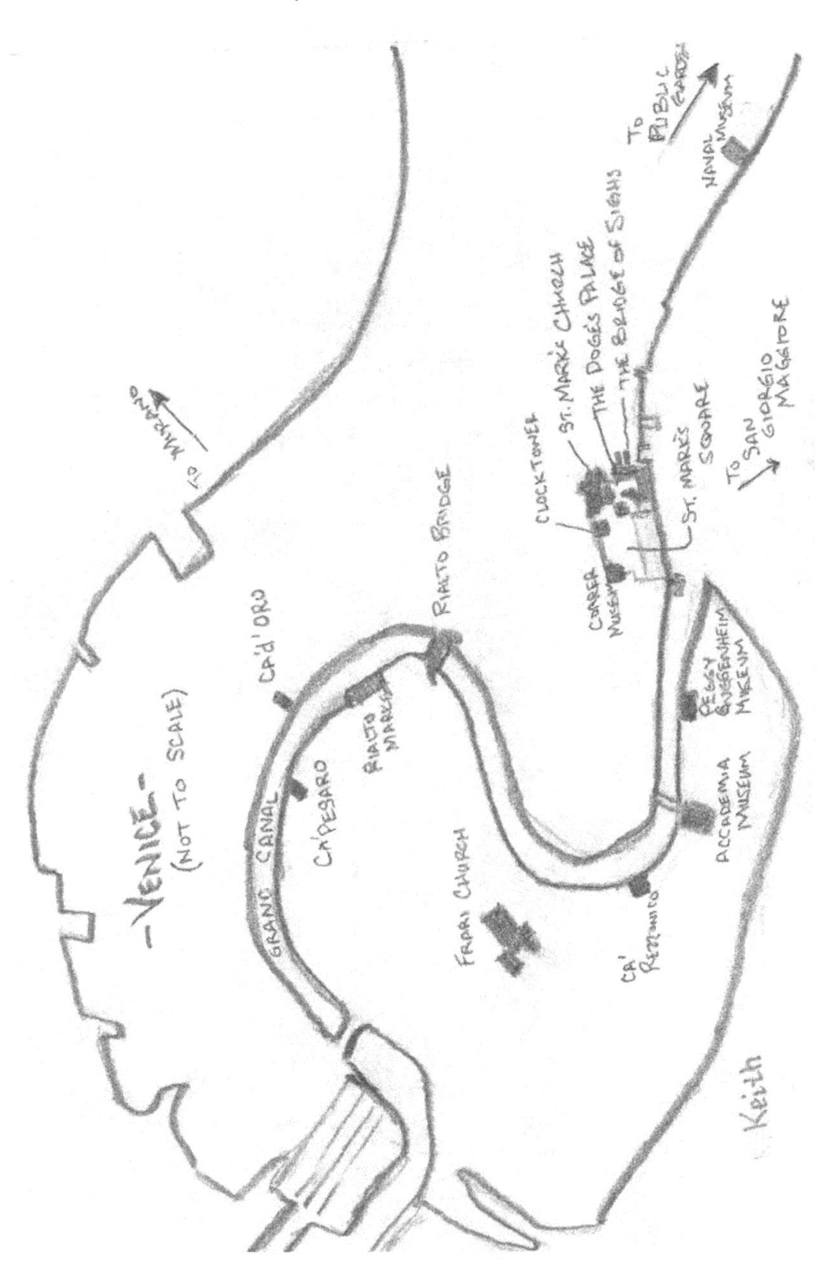

Map: St. Mark's Square

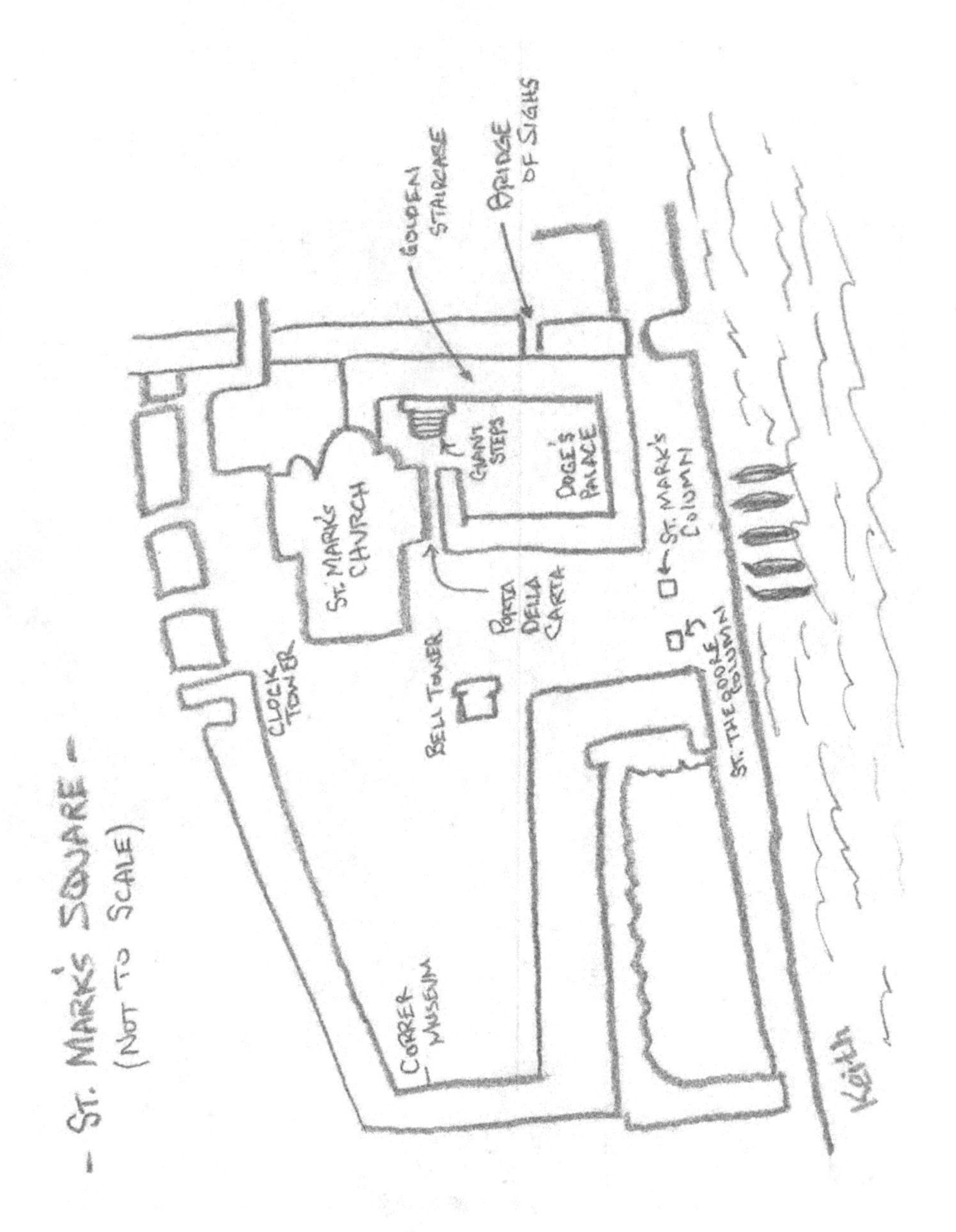

St. Mark's Maze

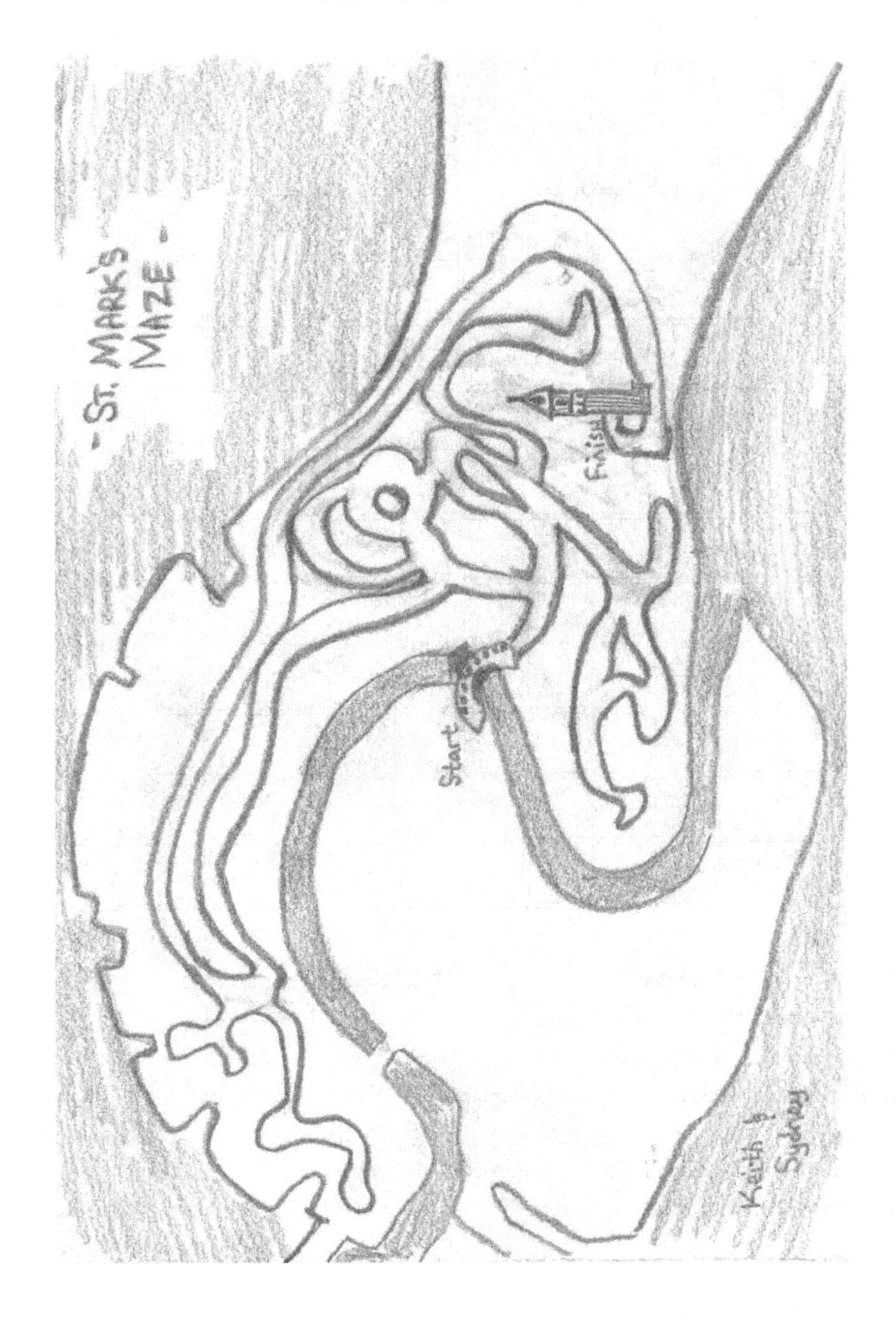

Crossword Venice

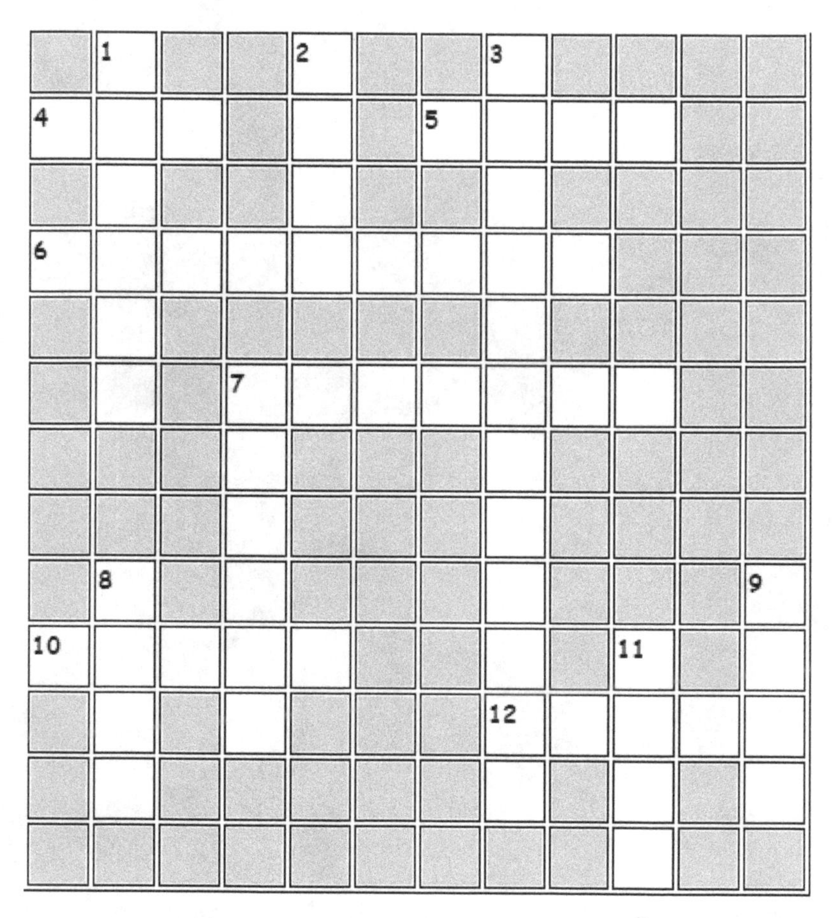

Across

4. Use one of these to keep cool
5. Winged animal is symbol of Venice
6. Famous young adventurer from Venice
7. A sleek black boat
10. These float and are all over Venice
12. Find this in Murano

Down

1. Cross these instead of streets
2. A beach in Venice
3. Famous bridge of Venice (2 words)
7. A cold treat to eat
8. The ruler of Venice was called this
9. Wear this during Carnival
11. Name of Patron Saint of Venice

Word Find Venice 1

Y	M	R	I	A	L	T	O	B	R	I	D	G	E	Z
K	V	L	M	M	Q	H	Z	U	G	D	G	E	H	G
C	O	G	X	V	M	E	U	X	Z	W	N	I	G	C
T	F	B	T	D	C	R	I	O	I	O	D	I	S	R
B	A	J	T	C	F	F	D	N	O	N	A	K	G	V
R	Q	D	T	A	S	B	G	G	V	N	A	T	V	E
E	J	U	V	N	E	E	A	A	T	K	L	M	G	V
I	D	J	N	A	D	L	P	S	C	S	O	O	L	D
L	Y	R	F	L	F	O	T	F	O	U	D	U	F	O
O	H	I	I	V	R	E	C	F	R	K	N	S	U	A
D	X	O	M	E	P	H	N	V	R	Y	O	U	R	N
N	N	Z	T	S	U	K	M	W	E	N	G	Z	M	V
O	O	T	X	R	C	A	L	E	R	Q	U	G	Y	Q
G	O	K	C	P	A	L	A	C	E	I	D	P	B	D
C	F	H	Y	Q	S	T	M	A	R	K	F	N	Y	D

CANAL
CHURCH
DOGE
GIANT STEPS
GONDOLA
GONDOLIER
LAGOON
PALACE
RIALTO BRIDGE
ST MARK
VAPORETTO
WINGED LION

Word Find Venice 2

X I W T B Y O A S G R F Z J P
M B Z F T N N C G U N K T Q X
Z A T F X C A S E A F O O D Z
P E R M A R R Q L S G Z O B U
R G X C N N U Z A S R D A Q P
O B K I O N M E T A I C X D A
B E V Q Q P S N O L F X A P S
H A R H I J O R W G S Y N D T
L Z N Z S J E L T Z Q K R A A
U H Z T I F R A O S C K I G Y
S A K M A S K U U W W I R Y G
E Z P Q X X G P B J L X T G T
A Y T Q K E T K B G E W J F T
O F U A N D S R S B S Z F G C
Y I C H I T T E H G A P S Q M

CARNIVAL	MASK
FAN	MURANO
GELATO	PASTA
GLASS	PIZZA
LIDO	SEAFOOD
MARCO POLO	SPAGHETTI

Word Find Venice 3

S	N	Z	J	K	J	D	P	I	T	Q	S	Q	A	Q
S	A	D	L	S	Q	O	K	P	M	N	W	T	A	I
V	I	H	O	U	N	W	Q	X	X	H	B	Z	K	A
I	T	P	A	T	S	M	U	E	S	U	M	E	S	N
S	I	R	E	H	M	J	R	M	W	R	Q	U	O	B
S	T	L	W	O	G	K	F	R	E	S	C	O	E	S
A	C	C	A	D	E	M	I	A	P	D	A	M	J	M
Z	V	B	E	F	W	T	M	Q	C	V	M	B	F	S
T	H	S	G	I	I	S	P	O	T	B	P	G	T	V
V	T	B	A	Q	U	F	G	I	S	U	A	P	R	G
D	Y	G	G	N	P	E	E	Z	G	A	N	M	N	M
Z	Z	Z	H	Z	M	O	L	O	P	E	I	T	C	B
R	G	I	R	A	R	F	Q	N	E	I	L	C	A	Z
J	A	Q	P	I	A	Z	Z	A	A	H	E	V	S	L
D	M	U	Q	X	R	G	T	N	I	Q	A	P	A	X

ACCADEMIA
ART
CAMPANILE
CASA
FRARI
FRESCOES
MOSAICS
MUSEUMS
PIAZZA
PONTE
TIEPOLO
TITIAN

Word Match

Draw a line to match the English word with the Italian word.

Venice	Gelato
Square	San Marco
Bridge	Piazza
Ice Cream	Venezia
Church	Ciao
Palace	Ponte
Saint Mark	Basilica
Goodbye	Palazzo